Twenty-One

Amirah Cowgill-Williams

BookLeaf Publishing

Presentation by *BookLeaf Publishing*

Web: www.bookleafpub.com

E-mail: info@bookleafpub.com

ISBN: 9789358367218

First edition 2023

I dedicate this book to my inner-child, my mom and my father, my sister and brother, my uncle Mike, the love of my life, and everyone who currently calls me friend or family.

I love you all more than words can express.

ACKNOWLEDGEMENT

I want to thank every single person who is currently in my life, family and friends.

I am inspired by each and every one of you (you should know who you are).

To every friend that treated me with love, and kindness.

To every family member, newly added or not, that has shown me full acceptance and love.

And to my readers, thank you for never giving up, and pushing through every adversity you have ever faced.

PREFACE

I decided to write this book as a challenge to myself, I wanted to see how far my creativity could take me during a certain amount of time, and I will say I surprised myself. I find my own poems to be intriguing and sometimes slightly humorous. I lowered my expectations of myself and let my creativity take the lead.

Glittery Eyes

My eyes glitter,
Through this storm I've weathered,
Oh, glittery eyes.

-Amirah WC

Human vs Mother Nature

When you feel, we feel,
We move to your beat
Do you cry from the sky when we cut away your
limbs?
The same way we cry, when someone we love,
says goodbye?
Or do we just call that rain?
Do you tip over sailboats in a fit of fury?
The same way we used to kick over Lincoln
Logs when we were upset?
Or do we just call those waves?
Do you huff and puff the same we do when
things don't go our way?
Or do we just call that the wind?
I know you never said you were perfect, you
never said you were always Zen
Just like us when we say, " I'm sorry, I'm
learning".
Our emotions are like your waves, they catch us
by surprise, is this human nature or mother
nature?
When the sun comes out does that mean you are
happy?
Or is that just clouds passing by?
And did you know we are resilient like you?

When war or famine comes our way, we double
down and rise up again,
Even more beautiful than before.
But I want to know, is this human nature or
mother nature?

-Amirah WC

To a Vanilla Infused Stout- A mesostic poem

Your aVerageness is low
    All should know
   VaNilla infused stout has my heart
   At fIrst I had my doubt
  I've Looked at them all, tried them too, but none were like you
     TaLl and dark you are (in my best Yoda voice)
     Admirable, delicious, and smooth

     I loved how strong your vanilla was and how much your hops were not
   aNd did you say you were also Bourbon Barreled aged?
  So Fun!
   I jUst loved the way you tasted
    Smooth, sweet and seductive
   nErvous as I write to you
    Despite knowing the truth, I still do

     Seeing you can't happen until summers through
   I'm Trying to say, I enjoyed my time with you
    yOu were the best beer I've tried

TrUe, silky and smooth
  sTout that is Vanilla Infused, I love you!

-Amirah WC

A Good Friend- a double acrostic poem

Almost silent, but the buzz of the bees by the
acadia
Go quietly, I say as you stand, as to not disturb
the bees buzzing
On my back, I watch the clouds drift on, then all
of the sudden I hear an achoo
Oh my! the bees are buzzing, you might scare
them away, I say with gusto
Don't disturb the bees please, and might I add
For the love of all that is good, would you like to
be disturbed? You stand aloof
Right, I say, bees make the color of this world,
so let them buzz through the air
I'm not saying the wasps, but gentle honey or
bumble bees, now pass the aoili
Eat with me my good friend, come sit by me
under this Acadia tree
No worries, no fear, just chillin' with the bees
buzzing on and on
Don't disturb the bees, but please stay with me
my good friend

-Amirah WC

Four Season Revelations

If you knew me then you would know
I was born in winter, but I rarely play in snow
And if I do I'm bundled warm
In my snow suit that's my truest form
Fall is my favorite, the color, the food
I feel so comforted, I'd hope you do too
Summer can suck it, that much is true
The heat, the bugs, I don't know about you
Springs just right, the colors, the vibes
I enjoy the air on my shoulders and the sun in
my eyes
The weather is wild, I enjoy the variation
But here are my revelations
21 years on this earth, I think its pretty clear
I enjoy fall time and a good dark beer
I enjoy sitting by a fire and watching
Claymation shows
And I barely tolerate summers heat, it goes by
really slow
Springs really pretty I enjoy watching the earth
be reborn
21 years on this earth, I think its pretty clear
I enjoy fall time and a good dark beer

-Amirah WC

Dear inner child

Dear inner child
I know its been a while
Since I've acknowledged you by name
I want you to know that you are always in my
heart
We are never far apart
Have you noticed the color starting to re-enter
my life?
Or how I no longer cry myself to sleep at night?
And did you notice how much more I truly
smile?
I know, its been a while
I've sat with you through the tears,
But have you noticed that even after all of these
years
When you cry that I'm still here?
I hear you whisper in my ear when someone has
a wacky opinion
About how you disapprove
And I bet you notice how I drown you out to
prove
That when you listen to understand and not to
just respond
You'll meet lots of people that you love for long
I know I wasn't true to myself for a while

I was a dim light and to be honest even though I
smiled
I was just going through a trial
And I almost let it win
Because for a long time I hated my own skin
I wanted to change who I was within
So I looked to you,
And even though I am learning to love myself
As much as I love others if not more
I look to you, yes you, the little girl who has
been there
The one who has held all of my fears
And overcame them
You soothe me in my time of need
And remind me that my love is pure and deep
You remind me what it feels like to be alive
To run my hand through the sand,
Feel the wind on my face
Or walk barefoot on this land
And to give myself grace
You remind me to express myself
You teach my confidence
To love this skin I'm in
And to have more tolerance
Dear inner child, even though its been a while
I am still here, there's no need to fear
I will hold your hand for the rest of my life
I will soothe you, even at night
I cant thank you enough for what you do

Just being yourself through and through
For teaching me, even now
During these little trials
What it means to feel alive even for a little while
Dear inner child, I'll always hold you near
And live my life as I wanted all those past years

- Amirah WC

Anxiety- what it feels like for me

Anxiety,
I start to sweat
And it makes me regret
Not being more positive before
I take a deep breath
My heart starts to flutter
If only I can take another..
"Breathe", you say to me.
Yet, I can feel it take over
Anxiety
My heart starts to get tighter and tighter
I have to try to breathe
I rub my chest
"Breathe", you say to me.
You get a little louder
"Breathe", you say to me.
I take a deep breath
But I falter
Anxiety
I feel heavy, gravity pulls me down
My eyes won't open
In my tears I drown
When it creeps up to my chest
It makes me sweat

My brain tells me its best
To just take it
This is my pain, I cant fake it
Anxiety
"Breathe", you say to me
I don't want to feel this
I feel caged
I cant take it anymore,
You pull me up from the floor
And I let you take over me
Perseverance
I start to move with you
Because if I don't then
How can I ever be free
If when I feel it creep
I sink with gravity?
With this I've lived my whole life
Anxiety and I have strife
Stripped in the middle of winter,
Sweat through my clothes
Fall to the ground
And beg to be freed
From this cage of anxiety
I have learned from you
I have learned that when I push through deep
breaths
What follows is often rest
Of my tight heart and what's not far
Is the slowness of my breath

What often follows is rest
Anxiety
I've learned to feel, to move with you
Perseverance

- Amirah WC

Instagram- A double acrostic

I scroll for hours and wonder why I can't look
that good in something that mini Never do I stop
to think of the great things I have to offer, I
never take the action
Something so small, like removing those who
make me question my worthiness
To fill my feed with positive things that let me
see how great I am, tears erupt
Again, I scrolled, and compared, but I know that
Instagram is just an ana
Given to us to gain popularity and to find people
who find us adoring
Realness is rare in this day in age, sometimes
Instagram feels like gasping for air
Any day now I will learn that I have so much to
offer, Instagram is just an ana
My hope is that Instagram can bring us together
and cause no harm

- Amirah WC

Bittersweet tears- a poem for the ones who have gone

Bittersweet tears
I welcome you here, this is a safe space
its been far too long since you've been gone and
I often feel this way
bittersweet tears
I want you to know, I'm just feeling a little sad
sad that I didn't get more time
but happy for the time that was mine
bittersweet tears as I picture you here, laughing
once more
bittersweet tears as I reminisce the time I had
with you
to watch you smile, a smile that went for miles
and a laugh that filled up a room
I cry these bittersweet tears because I am sad
you're no longer here
and that my time was cut short
I love you so and I want you to know
these tears are sad and true
but they're filled with love and happiness too
love that I got to share with you
these bittersweet tears, I welcome you here
this is a safe place.

-Amirah WC

I love for you- a poem for the siblings in my life

I want you to know
no matter how far you go
that I love you
I love to watch you grow
and my feelings for you overflow
into the universe
no matter where you are
or if you live really far
you are still a big piece of my heart
growing older is weird
honestly, it used to be one of my fears
but then I remembered I get to grow with you
watch you go on your own path
and help guide you
I love you
when life seems strange
and everything is in a haze
just know
I love you
and if tomorrow doesn't come fast enough
and it makes you feel glum
just know that
I love you

-Amirah WC

Matriarch

I am matriarch
I give life
from the moment I thought you up, you were
mine
I am matriarch
I will always take care of you so
you'll never have to wonder if you're enough
even though you're not here yet, I love you like
you are
I am matriarch
I gave you life
from the moment I thought you up, you were
mine
my body is strong, it knows what to do
to bring you in this world, this much is true
I am matriarch just so you know
you'll never have to wonder
I'll always love you so

-Amirah WC

Amirah

I am resilient
more than you'd ever think
even through a storm I stand up straight
I push through adversity
I am fierce
I walk with fire in my heart
I stand for what I love and I never back down
when I'm with the ones I love they'll never
frown
I am soft
I'll hold you tight
when you need me, I'll show you everything's
alright
I am vibrant
I shine through life, my smile is radiant
I love city lights
they make me feel inspired
I can dance the night away
or curl up with a good book
exploring is my middle name
I am strong
I am wise
my aura is clear
who am I?

-Amirah WC

Washington

The river makes a swoosh, as I run my hand
through Adam's Ale
a lovely sound to hear as I gaze up and see deer
dancing by
mountains big and small, make you wonder
who's walked that far
it makes you want to follow
trees sway softly, nourishing our lungs, it's a
give and take between us
bees fly around, attracting the color to the scene
so the pretty tulips you see can be all spring
a garden that brings all of our nutritional needs
with native plants for miles to see
and we know Dandelions are not bad weeds
water at nearly exit, this place so often feels like
heaven
with trees that cascade over you as you drive,
like a scene from a picture show
creating a shade and shadows that sway in the
sky, and wind that always flows
with moss on cliffs way up high, so soft you'll
drift off
and when you wake you will see, the ocean in
circulation
and the sun saying its ceremonious goodnight

If you're brave you can climb without even
knowing
up a cliff that isn't even showing
but when you look down you'll undoubtedly be
knowing
that you have to keep going
so much wildlife, it would shock you to see
all the things you thought you'd have to travel
far to see
the aquatic life is beautiful, the water always
sings
with orcas, whales dolphins and sea stars
Its full of life and mysteries
where small towns intertwine with the roads
that lead you to a glittering city
it leaves you inspired for days to come
so much to do, so much to see, trails that lead
you to places to be
the ones that overlook towns, and cities that
makes you feel really big
this state is unlike any other
full of adventure and wonder
Washington

-Amirah WC

Manifest

I manifest as easily as I breathe
all that I want comes to me
when I'm full of doubt, then I know
I'm not on a path that aligns with my soul
all the things my heart desires
come to me with ease
without thinking of the next step
I trust in divine timing
I know clear as day that when I know what I
don't want
I put what I do want in my way
trusting my inner being
for they know the way
they are my best self
on any given day
when I have doubt I bet my inner being says
"why don't you trust me yet?"
I'm so often put in my place when the universe
shows me
I'm not in the right place
I take a deep breath and force my thoughts to
change
for if I don't, I'll never see a day where
everything goes my way
I manifest as easily as I breathe

all I want comes to me, effortlessly.

-Amirah WC

Abraham Hicks- an acrostic poem

Align yourself with what's meant to be
Believing in what you want, and fully believing
it will come
Realizing when you're not in the right space to
truly accept what you want
Actively making the decision to think in a more
positive manner
Having the strength to accept where you are, not
trying to force change
Acknowledging when you think positive, you
attract it, and the latter is true
Making a difference by getting on a path that
makes you feel good

Holding space for yourself to feel and accepting
where you stand
In your mind you hold the power
Can you feel how your vibration changed when
you learn to name emotions?
Killing off the need to force change, letting the
universe guide you
See a change in life, when you accept where you
are, and follow the light

-Amirah WC

Silence

Silence for me is sitting under a tree and staring
off in the grass
wondering if that ant is on his way home from
work
I wonder when he's off is he's full of sass
and if his any wife just gives him a task and is a
bit of jerk
silence for me is sitting on a giant rock by the
ocean
and listening to the waves
it brings up a sort of emotion
that if I sit long enough, that emotion remains
silence for me is sitting next to you, not a word
drifts through the air
I am peaceful and calm as I run my fingers
through your hair
never for a moment do I wish you weren't there
silence is sitting in the shower and feeling the
water drip down my body
closing my eyes, to feel my hair fill with water
silence is in the morning, right when I wake
thinking of good things, to start off my day
silence for me can also be the latter
depending on the day

but I have found many ways to force myself to
say, what I may need to say
to get through those tough days
most days, I'd just say I can be silent and that's
okay

-Amirah WC

Flowers- a poem from two perspectives

I got flowers today, I thought it was swell
I know who sent them, you could really tell
I sent her flowers today I tried really hard
I know she knows who sent them that far
I got flowers today, this was really sweet
you can tell he tried to make them really neat
I sent her flowers today and I didn't go to the
store
but I crouched way down and watched out for
thorns
I got flowers today, and they were really fresh
when I shook them a little from the root dirt fell
I sent her flowers today and I wanted her to
know
they were super fresh, I assume dirt got on her
floor
I got flowers today, and it didn't come with a
note
but I think I know who sent it and where he
wants to go
I sent her flowers today, but I didn't leave a note
she know who I am and where I want to go
I got flowers today, and for a moment it felt
really special

but again he's just not on my level
I sent her flowers today, I want her to know
I miss her so

-Amirah WC

A dream within a dream

I run my fingers through the field of poppies
The petals feel soft, but strong
I peek inside to see the golden pollen
and I see a little sleeping bug
I smile to myself, because this moment is so
simple
I walk some more, careful to avoid any flowers
as I walk, I start to notice
the field turn into a trail lined with rose bushes
the roses are singing, I wonder if I am dreaming
I feel like the little prince
"come hither", they say, "we smell divine, come
feel how soft our petals are"
I run my fingers through the bushes,
forgetting about the thorns until my fingers run
over one
"ouch", I say," you're beautiful, but you've
caused me pain "
"you have to be delicate with us", they respond
"or maybe I can just cut your thorns off", I say
"no way", the roses say," please, if you cant love
us for us, just leave"
I walk some more, avoiding these bushes
for as pretty as they are, I'm sure this will leave a
scar

as I keep walking, I start to notice a forest, the
trees aren't frozen
they're dancing with each other, I can feel the
love
roots from beneath send music up above
I walk into the forest and this is what they say
"human, human please don't cut us down"
"'we are just dancing, please keep our kin safe
and sound"
I look to my left and what do I see?
little baby trees sleeping peacefully
I respond, "no worries about me trees, please go
back to dancing for me"
they smile and wave their branches, and go back
to doing the sway
I walk through the forest and what do I see?
A field of lavender, smelling as good as can be
I walk through the field stopping at every flower
taking it in for about an hour
then all of a sudden, I start to feel sleepy
oh I forgot, lavender was good at creeping
creeping peacefully until you are sleeping
I lay down in the field of lavender dreams
and what I dreamt of could have kept me asleep
The perfect place just for me, trees barren with
fruit
bushes blooming with flora
trees that like to sing and dance, with their kin
sleeping peacefully by

I look up at the sky and its painted swirls of blue
and white
I just might cry, but did I mention this place
while it feels like heaven
also feels so familiar?
I walk around some more when I hear a moo, I
look to my left and smile
I see a little baby cow waddling by
all the farm animals I desire, on a hill, no city
lights for miles
the sun it sets, every night, leaving colors from
the day lingering by
and when it goes away the sky fills up with stars
twinkling on
one comes to me, but I don't get scared
I feel a familiar soul, I feel he is near
he shines on down, and smiles at my face, I feel
his warmth
the cane, the guitar, a laugh that's so free
He smiles at me, and as quickly as he came, he
says
" I must go now the star says to me, it's almost
my time to shine don't you see,
the pattern of the night within me"
I watch as the soul flies up to the sky, and I lay
there wondering, wondering why
I drift asleep again in these fields
but when I wake in the morning, as I reach for
the flowers

I notice they aren't there
instead I knock over water on my nightstand
I look around and what do I see?
I'm in my room as safe as can be
I look out my window and to my surprise
I see a field of poppies, not very high
I look to the left and I see a calf that waddles
trees that dance and roses that sing
and I realize in that moment, life is a dream
within a dream

- Amirah WC

I got upset today

I got upset today, it was a feeling that I felt in
my veins
usually I bust out and say " hey, I am angry
today, you made me this way"
I've grown since those times, where I would be
angry
and it would stay on my mind
but I took a deep breath
and I thought about something positive, and
chose not to receive,
the negative energy you were bringing around
me
I got upset today, but I was soft with my words
for even when I hurt, I lead with the heart
I got upset today and I handled it with grace
I proud of myself, I got upset today.

-Amirah WC

Friendship

When we were children, it was so easy to see
friends that were perfect, loving and care free
the games we played, took much imagination,
the love between us never had an end destination
when we were teens, vision got foggy
we just wanted to be loved
and have friends that were fond of us
the friendships we chose were so deep and real
that when we would lose one, it took a while for
our heart to heal
these people were fun-loving and adventurous
and when we really needed them, they
understood us
Now we are older, and life has been moving fast
gone are some of the friendships we've had in
the past
some of these lessons, taught us to be better
better at picking the company we keep
because the people we had were a reflection of
what we chose to think
the friends we have now are ones for life
through the shared experiences and life lessons
to teach
without the craziness our adult friends we love
to keep

as an adult its easier to see
friendship isn't tricky, and it shouldn't be
the people we allow to sit with us
are a reflection of what we believe
so now we choose our friends wisely in order to
keep
the love and support for years to come
The bond of friendship can't be broken
it's a love that's always spoken

-Amirah WC

Growth

My identity, I do not know, but I'm learning as I
go
I'm accepting the skin I'm in, well learning to, as
I grow
My growth is never ending, just so you know
the knowledge within me is always expanding
when I acknowledge my own growth its a sign
of perseverance
when I was my lowest, I almost couldn't see
for the hole I dug myself was about 10 ft deep
I had to make a choice to want better for myself
a couple of times deeper I fell
one thing I can say, is that perseverance is
something I've carried all the way
and here I am another day
breathing and living life
one day at a time
picking a path that is fully mine
one thing for certain, that I know
is that growth is never-ending
nor a one man show
with every action we take to better ourselves
we are introducing positive growth to our cells
a new life we forge as we move forward again
new growth will happen, I promise, my friend

- Amirah WC

www.ingramcontent.com/pod-product-compliance
Lightning Source LLC
La Vergne TN
LVHW010924200726
843509LV00013B/2059